A BUDDHIST
MANIFESTO

A BUDDHIST MANIFESTO
THE PRINCIPLES OF THE **TRIRATNA** BUDDHIST COMMUNITY

SUBHUTI

Print copies of this book are available at:
http://tinyurl.com/buddhistmanifesto
And as a free pdf:
http://tinyurl.com/buddhistmanifesto2

Published by
Triratna Liaison Office
Madhyamaloka
30 Chantry Road
Birmingham B13 8DH

ISBN: 978-1-4717-7207-8
©
Dharmachari Subhuti 2012

The right of Dharmachari Subhuti to be identified as the author of this work has been asserted by him in accordance with the Copyright, Designs and Patents Act 1988

Contents

vii	*Foreword by Urgyen Sangharakshita*
1	I: The Principles of the Triratna Buddhist Community
3	II: Going for Refuge to the Three Jewels
7	III: Going for Refuge to the Buddha
11	IV: Going for Refuge to the Dharma
23	V: Going for Refuge to the Sangha
43	VI: The Principles of a Buddhist Renewal
44	*Further information*

Foreword
by Urgyen Sangharakshita

When I founded what is now the Triratna Buddhist Community in 1967, I did so after many years experience of Buddhism in the East and some two or three of the nascent Buddhist movement in Britain. I had of course seen much that inspired me and I had met many good Buddhists and some great ones, some of whom indeed became my teachers. However, I had also witnessed much more that was corrupt or decadent and much that simply had no relevance to the modern situation. It had become clear to me that, in many respects, a completely new start was required if the Dharma was to survive at all, let alone make any impact in the contemporary world. I came to this conclusion somewhat reluctantly, being by character something of a traditionalist. But I saw no alternative. Time has only reinforced my conclusion; indeed we must, I believe, be more radical still.

As I set out on this work of renewal, I found that certain principles were becoming clear to me as a basis for it, and these guided me in establishing the Triratna Buddhist Community. I believe these principles are applicable to all who work for the Dharma today and so wanted to bring them to the attention of other Buddhists worldwide. I am, however, now unable to write much myself, being partially sighted, and so I have asked one of my senior disciples, Dharmachari Subhuti, to give a brief synopsis of the main principles on the basis of which we work, as a sort of manifesto for modern Buddhism. Subhuti has been working with me for almost forty years and knows these principles very well, both in their theoretical depth and in their practical application. What he has written does indeed well summarise what I consider to be the essential basis for the renewal of Buddhism. I therefore commend it to my own disciples and to our Buddhist brothers and sisters everywhere. May it contribute to the flourishing of the Dharma throughout the world.

Urgyen Sangharakshita,
Madhyamaloka, Birmingham, UK
3rd June 2012

I
The Principles of the Triratna Buddhist Community

The Triratna Buddhist Community was founded by Urgyen Sangharakshita, in London in 1967, as a response to the contemporary world, so different in many ways from any that Buddhists have had to face before. What follows is an outline of the main principles upon which that new Buddhist movement was initiated and which have continued to animate it ever since. This is intended as an epitome of those principles, setting them out in brief, without much supporting exposition, so that their full range can be discerned.

THE NEED FOR A RENEWAL OF BUDDHISM
The world today is very different from that in which Buddhism originated and flourished. Buddhists now practise and teach the Dharma in an age of urbanisation, globalisation, mass communication, and rapid technological change, in which scientific thinking is widespread and ideas of democratic rights are common. In addition, the influence of Buddhism in its traditional heartlands has drastically decreased, especially through the course of the twentieth century. However, opportunities for propagating the Dharma are arising in new regions, most notably in India and in the West – and everywhere there are people with a cosmopolitan outlook and questioning minds to whom the Buddhist perspective would be naturally congenial. The

challenge Buddhists face today is to find ways of communicating and practising the Dharma that are truly effective in these new circumstances. **The situation seems to call for renewal in the Buddhist world, faithful to the Buddha's own teaching, yet addressing the circumstances we find ourselves in now.**

This work of renewal is very important to us in the Triratna Buddhist Order, but we know that it is not our work alone. We are aware that many other Buddhists all over the world are grappling with the same issues and we want to cooperate with them in this common task. Like all other schools and groups, we have our own distinctive approach to the teaching and practice of the Dharma, which we derive from the presentation of our teacher and founder, Urgyen Sangharakshita. At the same time we see ourselves as part of the worldwide Mahasangha of all those who go for Refuge to the Buddha, Dharma, and Sangha, in whatever manner and to whatever degree.

Our teacher has arrived at certain principles, which are the basis of our own approach to the practice of Buddhism today, however partially or imperfectly we have been able to apply them so far. We think these principles of renewal may be of wider interest and application and we therefore want to share them with our Buddhist sisters and brothers as a contribution to our common work of bringing the Dharma into the heart of the world today. We hope these principles will be stimulating, at least, and we invite your reflection and comment.

II
Going for Refuge to the Three Jewels

The renewal of the Buddhist world can only come about if it is faithful to the spirit and intention of the **Buddha's** own teaching. At the same time, it needs to find new ways of expressing the **Dharma** that are relevant to people today, without denying the rich variety of traditions and cultures of the Buddhist past. To carry this message of the Dharma out into the world, a nucleus of men and women is required, forming a new kind of **Sangha**, especially of effective Dharma teachers and leaders, firmly based in deep personal practice. That renewal of the Buddhist world is, in other words, a renewal of our understanding and expression of the **Buddha, Dharma, and Sangha** and a renewal of our **going for Refuge** to them. This, for us in the Triratna Buddhist Order, is the starting point.

The central and definitive act of the Buddhist life is going for Refuge to the Buddha, Dharma, and Sangha. All Buddhists, probably, would acknowledge that it is by reciting the formula of going for Refuge that one becomes a Buddhist and most will regularly chant it, together with one or other list of precepts, as a centrepiece of their devotional ceremonies. It is thus what most fundamentally we have in common as Buddhists and what distinguishes us from non-Buddhists.

But going for Refuge is not merely a ceremonial recitation: it defines and expresses what it is to be a Buddhist. When we go for Refuge to the Three Jewels, we express our confidence in them and our reliance upon them as the ultimate sources of happiness and fulfilment – and we implicitly reject all other sources of confidence and reliance, whether from the world of the senses or from other views. We are not only confident in the Three Jewels, our whole Dharma life unfolds on the basis of that confidence. We **go** for Refuge to them: we actively move in the direction they imply. Going for Refuge to the Three Jewels is an action, and it is repeated again and again until Enlightenment is reached.

However, initially our faith in the Three Jewels is only partial – whatever we may chant in the Dharma-hall, much of the time we look to other sources of security: people, material goods, worldly situations and status, various unquestioned views and beliefs. As we progress on the Path, our going for Refuge will move through a number of stages until it becomes complete. To begin with, our going for Refuge may simply be the expression of **cultural** values – a positive influence upon us but with little depth of personal reflection or commitment. At some point, we may catch a glimpse of the Dharma and make a temporary or **provisional** commitment. In time that may become **effective**, as we reorganise our lives around our commitment to the Three Jewels, so that we do make consistent progress on the Path. As we go for Refuge more and more deeply, our confidence in the Buddha, Dharma, and Sangha becomes unshakeable and we enter the stream of the Dharma, from which we cannot fall away. This is **real** going for Refuge and, from that moment on, our progress is assured, until we ourselves become the Refuge: our going for Refuge then being **Absolute**.

Going for Refuge is thus repeated again and again at every moment of our lives, carrying us through all the stages of the Path. It is this active faith, commitment, and effort that makes up the Buddhist life and is the starting point for any renewal of Buddhism – to be constantly repeated if the momentum of that renewal is not itself to be lost.

Although going for Refuge to the Three Jewels is the central and definitive act of the Buddhist life, different schools have drawn out important aspects of what it consists in through their own distinctive approaches. Some, for instance, have emphasised the Vinaya, others the Bodhisattva vow, others again the taking of tantric initiation, and yet others reliance on the vow of the Buddha Amitabha. All of these have their own particular relevance and meaning, enriching our understanding of the Dharma. But all find their unity as aspects and dimensions of going for Refuge to the Three Jewels. Recognition of them in these terms allows us to view Buddhism as one spiritual movement and makes it easier for us to work together and to communicate a single, basic message that can be widely effective in our contemporary situation.

Buddhist renewal commences with the recognition of the central significance of going for Refuge to the Three Jewels, at every level and in every aspect of Buddhist life.

III
Going for Refuge to the Buddha

Going for Refuge to the Three Jewels begins with going for Refuge to the Buddha. But who is the Buddha? Which Buddha do we go for Refuge to?

All Buddhists honour the historical Buddha Shakyamuni, but the various schools and traditions understand his role in diverse ways and assign him different positions. In large areas of the Buddhist world, Shakyamuni Buddha is given a place that is more or less secondary to other figures. For instance, in much Far Eastern Buddhism, the Buddha Amitabha has the pre-eminent position, while Tibetans will usually give prime honour to the founding gurus of their own schools, who are considered to have been Buddhas, and will also worship a rich pantheon of archetypal or visionary Buddhas and Bodhisattvas.

These figures have great spiritual relevance within those traditions – and it is important that their worship and contemplation is respected since they are embodiments of the essence of Enlightenment. However, they can be better understood and appreciated if they are placed carefully in relation to the Buddha Shakyamuni, in a way that reveals his full historical significance. Since the entire tradition emerges from his Enlightenment, we can most truly comprehend his teaching, and thereby discern our unity as Buddhists, when we see him as central. In addition, when we focus on the Buddha Shakyamuni, we make the Dharma more accessible to those who have had no previous contact with Buddhism by setting it within its historical context and demonstrating its relevance to them as human beings. For most people today, the gateway to the supra-historical is likely to be through history.

The Buddha Shakyamuni is the fountainhead of Buddhism. He rediscovered the Path and proclaimed it in this era. It is because of him that we know of the depths of Enlightenment represented by the visionary Buddhas and Bodhisattvas revealed in the Mahayana sutras and in the tantras – for they are expressions, on the level of uplifted imagination, of the spiritual wealth of the Enlightenment that he rediscovered. They themselves therefore find their significance through him. Indeed, the danger is that, without the historical context of Shakyamuni's Enlightenment, they come to be seen as mere god-figures, available for the magical manipulation of worldly life. This is all too commonly the case in traditional Buddhism today.

It is similarly important that the great gurus who founded particular schools are seen in a proper relationship to Shakyamuni. Such pre-eminent teachers have made enormous contributions to the tradition and are worthy of being honoured very highly indeed and their teachings studied very carefully. They are all, however, disciples of the Buddha himself and their particular presentations of the Dharma are explanations, explorations, or expansions of what he taught. Recognising this enables us to locate their teachings in the context of what the Buddha himself had to say and prevents us from losing the unity of the tradition through basing ourselves on relatively late approaches to the Dharma that are specific to certain historical and doctrinal circumstances.

A renewal of Buddhism starts with the Buddha Shakyamuni and his teachings, before the doctrinal developments of them that are so prominent in many schools. These later developments are not, however, necessarily to be discarded, by any means: they may contain teachings and practices that are very relevant today. A renewed Buddhism cannot be merely fundamentalist, purporting to maintain the authentic tradition unchanged since the time of the Buddha – that would be to ignore the vastly different circumstances we must practise in today and to waste the wealth of later spiritual experience, as well as to raise very large questions concerning historical evidence.

The starting point is as near as we can get to the Buddha himself and to what it seems almost certain that he did teach, found in the core of very early scriptures, preserved principally in the *nikāyas* of the Pali canon and in the *āgamas*, found in the Chinese canon and other such sources, mostly translated from the Sanskrit. This does not at all deny the value of later material but, insofar as it is later, it is a development on that core of the Buddha's own teaching and can only be fully understood, judged, and valued from that standpoint.

The Buddha to whom we go for Refuge is, in the first place, the founder of our traditions: the human, historical Shakyamuni. Seeing him as the primary object of Refuge allows us to make sense of developments that have taken place since his time; it enables us to appreciate the significance of the supra-historical, visionary figures that have emerged as expressions of the inner qualities of the Enlightenment he rediscovered; and it communicates clearly the inspiring potential that all human beings have. What is distinctive about Buddhism is that it offers us a vision of the highest possibilities that are open to humanity. The Buddha started as a human being, like us, and what he did we can do.

IV
Going for Refuge to the Dharma

The Dharma is the way things truly are, beyond all ordinary understanding, and it is by realising the Dharma directly for himself that Gautama became the Buddha Shakyamuni. Having achieved Liberation, the Buddha passed the remainder of his life communicating to others his fundamental insight into the nature of reality and teaching the Path that would lead them to share it. The Dharma is therefore also the body of teachings, practices, and institutions that constitute that Path to Enlightenment, based originally on the Buddha's own words.

On this much, all Buddhists can presumably, in essence, agree. But many different expressions of the Dharma have developed over the millennia, some of them, it would seem, mutually contradictory. This wealth, vast and various as it is both in its geographical breadth and its historical depth, is becoming available to us now as it has been to no Buddhists ever before. Modern Buddhists are, then, faced with the task of evaluating two thousand five hundred years of Buddhist development across much of Asia. We must distinguish what is true to the Dharma in that development from what is distorted or merely adventitious. We cannot accept uncritically everything that carries the label, 'Buddhist', from no matter what era or clime, because there is so much that is incidental or erroneous. Yet we cannot reject all but what belongs to one particular school – no modern school can be accepted as a 'pure tradition', unchanged since the time of the Buddha, no matter what its adherents might claim.

VALUING MODERN SCHOLARSHIP

Modern historical scholarship, which has contributed very significantly to our awareness of Buddhism's extent, offers a way forward. We can now gain some perspective, with growing accuracy, on how different schools came about in response to particular circumstances. **We can view the Buddhist tradition itself as a conditioned phenomenon, subject to the laws of dependent arising – of change, decay, and renewal – as the Buddha taught us that everything is.**

Buddhism has nothing to be afraid of in this respect: while Judaism, Christianity, and Islam, for the most part, rest upon the divine origins of their holy books, Buddhists can accept that, like all other things, the Tripitaka itself and the teachings it contains arose in dependence on conditions. We have access to far more accurate historical and philological knowledge about the origins and nature of the Buddhist texts we have inherited than has been available since they were created. Even if this knowledge sometimes tends to undermine the traditional accounts of how the texts came about, it does not destroy their Dharmic worth as teachings about the goal and the Path. Once we have removed the veils of a shallow 'sacredness', we can better understand how and why we have got what now comes down to us and therefore can more easily assess its value to us now.

ADAPTATION, CREATIVE UNFOLDING, AND INTERNAL RENEWAL IN THE TRADITION

When we look at the tradition as a whole, from this point of view, we see three principal processes at work. The Buddha communicated the

Dharma at a particular point in time against the background of particular cultural, economic, and political circumstances. While much that he said, as it has come down to us, requires no modification, he could not have spoken for all times and all places in the detail of his communication. The Buddha's successors have had to **adapt to new circumstances**, especially as they encountered new cultures outside India, and have had to evolve new and appropriate ways of expressing the essential truths of the Dharma. Faithfulness to the Dharma does not mean merely preserving and continuing the forms in which it was originally presented – which would, ironically, be a form of bad faith. The tradition also evolved in many different directions as fresh Dharmic inspiration arose within it. Even the Buddha's own teaching could not exhaust the infinite possibilities of the Dharma. The greatest of the Buddha's heirs have unfolded more of the Dharma's riches from their own **creative experience**. New dimensions of the truth have been revealed and more effective and uplifting ways of conveying it have developed. These new insights and expressions have helped to shape much of what we see in modern Buddhism.

Another process has also contributed to the rich variety of schools and traditions. Buddhism is not only in dialogue with the ever changing world around it, it is **in dialogue with itself**. There is an inevitable process of decay within the tradition, as power and status assert themselves, as misunderstandings become institutionalised, as one-sided emphases take on concrete form. These degenerations are also represented in the overall tradition as it comes down to us today. But so are the teachings that developed in order to correct them. **The tradition as a whole preserves those traces of decay as well as the signs of correction and renewal.**

A CRITICAL ECUMENICISM

On this basis, we may establish the criteria for the Dharma in the present age. We can take an ecumenical approach, open to the totality of Buddhist tradition – but ecumenicism does not preclude intelligent discrimination: a **critical ecumenicism** is what is called for. What has come down to us has been subject to the processes of adaptation to new situations, of creative evolution, of degeneration and renewal. We can find much that is of great value everywhere in this inheritance, but what is valuable to us is to be distinguished from what is merely incidental, contaminated with non-Buddhist ideas, or even degenerate. But what is the touchstone of value? Scholarly research can help us here too, because it enables us to discern with a reasonable degree of accuracy what are the earliest texts that are most likely to represent something close to the Buddha's own words – although we can never be completely certain that we are encountering exactly the words he used or that we have an exhaustive account of what he said. These earliest texts contain all the basic teachings that are accepted by all schools and traditions. **This then gives us a basis for evaluating whether or not later developments are authentic expressions of the Dharma: do they conform to or conflict with what the Buddha himself taught, as represented by that earliest corpus of teachings?** The issue here is not whether or not the teaching is *formally* the same as what the Buddha taught, but whether or not it conforms to it in principle.

However, this test is not enough. Simply because a later teaching or practice does not conflict with what the Buddha taught does not mean it is useful. So much that is no longer spiritually efficacious might be preserved under that criterion. We need to see whether those later developments are really helpful now, as means of communicating the Buddha's understanding. Considering the situation in the world today, we have no time to waste in simply preserving the past. We need a presentation of the Dharma that will really work now to change the lives of many people.

We can base our presentation of the Dharma firmly on the core teachings of the Buddha himself and include whatever from any traditional source is found to be effective and in conformity with what we know the Buddha taught. It may also include new ways of communicating the teachings that emerge from the present situation – so long, again, as they are in conformity with the principles contained in the Buddha's own words.

NEITHER ETERNALIST NOR NIHILIST

The most important basic doctrinal criterion for evaluating teachings is the extent to which they conform to the Middle Way, taught by the Buddha as avoiding the extremes of eternalism and nihilism. His teaching represented a complete break with his Indian religious and intellectual background, which was one of intense metaphysical speculation. He himself rigorously resisted all such theorising beyond what was necessary to follow the Path and attain the Goal and fought a continuous battle against all kinds of speculative views, which he considered distracted from the task in hand or, worse, led astray, ethically and spiritually. His teaching of dependent arising points to the observable characteristic shared by all things, rather than to an ultimate reality within which all takes place or which is their true meaning. He considered such 'eternalist' views as leading easily to very negative ethical and spiritual consequences. He was not however a nihilist or materialist, which he saw as, if anything, more pernicious. He taught, from his own experience, that it is possible to follow a sequence of dependently arising states that leads to Liberation, the ultimate and most desirable good.

While no modern schools would deny the central importance of the Middle Way, especially as represented by the teaching of dependent arising, some of the ways the Dharma is discussed can stray towards one or other extreme. The trend seems to have started quite soon after the Buddha's own Parinirvana, with the attempt to systematise his teachings, which in some cases fell into a quasi-realism. As time went on this trend became stronger and, in some later Mahayana and Vajrayana sources, there is terminology that suggests eternal metaphysical entities, even if that is not what was originally intended. There has been a contrary trend in other schools towards presenting the Buddha's teaching in such a one-sidedly negative fashion, effectively as the denial of all life and feeling, that it becomes deeply unappealing. Both this quasi-eternalism and quasi-nihilism lose the spirit of the Buddha's own message. Whatever the intention or understanding of their exponents, they slip away from the Middle Way.

The problem seems to have been that the full significance of dependent arising was not always appreciated. In many cases, even today, it is understood as referring simply to the chain of conditions that underlie our bondage in Samsara: the twelve-fold *nidāna* chain. The escape from Samsara is presented merely as the negation or undoing of these twelve links. Later traditions have tried to compensate for this rather bleak perspective through metaphysical explorations that sometimes rely on terms that have an inescapably eternalist ring, if not understood correctly, whatever their original intention.

The whole Buddhist tradition emerges out of the Buddha's own fundamental insight into the conditioned nature of all things. If this is understood and presented correctly no more is required – indeed, 'more' often leads inexorably in the direction of eternalism or nihilism. Dependent arising includes both the cycles of Samsara and the spiralling progression of the Path that leads to Nirvana. Nirvana arises as the expositional end point of the sequence of dependently arising states that constitute the Path – it is the point at which language is finally defied, though it implies no stopping point. That sequence is dealt with in various ways in the Buddha's own teaching: for instance, as the three trainings of *śīla*, *samādhi*, and *prajñā* – the Buddha's main topic during his last teaching journey. Most importantly, the Buddha discusses twelve progressive *nidānas* that lead to Liberation in two suttas of the Pali canon that seem largely to have escaped notice (see especially the *Upanisa Sutta*, Samyutta Nikāya, XII.23). Later traditions have their own sequences of dependently arising progressions, such as the ten Bodhisattva *bhūmis* or the various stages detailed in Vajrayana traditions, such as the Nine Yanas of the Nyingmapa – although these are not generally discussed in terms of dependent arising.

Dependent arising then does not merely characterise the chain that binds us to suffering. It includes also the Path by which we can escape from suffering. The total complex of conditioned processes includes two principal trends: a Samsaric and a Nirvanic. The Nirvanic trend is driven first of all by **skilful karma**. As we act more and more skilfully, more and more refined and sensitive states of mind emerge, which support a greater recognition of the truth. Once we see things as they really are at Stream Entry, a **Dharmic trend** takes over – we enter a stream that carries us on to Nirvana. What happens beyond Nirvana exhausts our understanding, but it should not be conceived either in eternalist or nihilist terms – at this point one can only have recourse to paradox or to symbol and myth.

All later teachings on the subject of the way things are can be tested against the Buddha's fundamental expression of his insight, the doctrine of dependent arising, seen in its fullness as encompassing both Samsara and Nirvana. This is the doctrinal departure point for a renewal of Buddhism.

A BALANCED APPROACH TO THE PRACTICE OF THE DHARMA

It is important that practice of the Dharma is balanced if it is to be relevant and effective in contemporary circumstances. Different schools within Buddhism have preserved different spiritual currents, many of which are significant for us today. Often these take the form of emphases on one or other aspect of Dharma teaching or practice. In traditional contexts these emphases have, at best, taken their place within a larger Buddhist culture that contained other balancing emphases. With the radical cultural shifts that have taken place worldwide in recent times, in which old patterns are being drastically eroded, traditional schools can be left with rather one-sided presentations. Some, for instance, emphasise study of the scriptures and commentaries at the expense of meditation, while others place so much importance on meditation that study is virtually excluded. Others again give priority to ritual and ceremony, to following Vinaya rules and precepts, or to practical work, often minimising the importance of other aspects. Sometimes also, exclusive emphasis is given to one or other particular way of practising or one technique, which is claimed as the true and correct one, whether taught by the Buddha or a later teacher.

No particular practice or technique is supreme or universal. **Following the Path demands a total transformation of all aspects of the individual and that requires a balanced approach that will include a range of practices.** In addition, at different stages of growth or under varying circumstances, the pattern of practice will probably need to change. What practices are engaged with by any individual will require constant monitoring to see that they are truly supporting development on the Path. One of the functions of Sangha, as we shall see later, is to ensure that each member is truly growing in the Dharma and growing in a balanced way.

One of the most important balances to be struck is that between personal transformation and altruistic activity. The Buddhist life is lived for the attainment of Bodhi, which consists in the final transcendence of all ego-clinging. The first and most important stage in real spiritual evolution is Stream Entry, when that ego-clinging is decisively broken. Once one lets go of that self-attachment, what is released is a stream of mental states that have less and less reference to self. In a phrase, what is unleashed once Insight is attained is selfless compassion. Striving for Enlightenment then must balance that quest for direct understanding of the unreal nature of the assumed metaphysical self with active giving up of self to the service of the Dharma and, thereby, of all life. A one-sided stress on one or the other will distort spiritual practice and thereby limit its success.

RESTORING THE REALM OF IMAGINATION

Modern Buddhists face another very challenging issue. Traditionally Buddhists have accepted a rich and complex perspective on life, seeing existence peopled by incalculable numbers of sentient beings: beings such as animals and insects that occupy the same material world as us, as well as beings occupying other world-systems elsewhere in space. More especially, the tradition takes for granted a vast and complex array of spirits, demons, angels, gods, together with archetypal beings or visionary Buddhas and Bodhisattvas, occupying other dimensions parallel to ours, sometimes overlapping with it.

Existence has traditionally been viewed as stratified into layers of worlds of increasing subtlety and beauty, each with its own laws of space and time. From the Buddha's own day on, the existence of these beings and dimensions has been accepted quite literally.

Such beings and realms are integral to the Dharma as traditionally expressed, but they are in direct conflict with the prevailing 'scientific' world-view, which is predominantly materialist. What is modern Buddhism to make of this conflict between the traditional world-view and the one that is widely current?

There is little doubt that quite a bit of Buddhist culture could usefully be subjected to critical enquiry. A great deal of credulity and superstition encrusts what has come down to us and a quest for evidence and an examination of sources would clear away a great deal of cant. While much of this sort of material is colourful and engaging, there is quite a lot that encourages credulity, and perpetuates superstition and ignorance, which can all too easily be exploited by powerful interests and often, for instance, obstructs real social reform. However, truth is not merely of the five physical senses. It is integral to the Dharma that worlds beyond the senses exist – although we need a new language to speak of these worlds and a deeper ontology to understand the nature of their existence. **A key task for Buddhist renewal is to forge a language and ontology that finds a Middle Way between the superstition and ignorance so common in tradition and the reductive materialism of popular scientism.** The language of Imagination offers an immediate starting point for that process. Besides this philosophical task, there needs to be a renewed exploration of these dimensions from within our modern cultures. The primary means for such exploration is through the direct experience of meditation. However, an important and more widely accessible means is available to us through art.

THE SIGNIFICANCE OF ART AND CULTURE

Buddhism has an exceptionally rich artistic and cultural history. We have inherited a vast wealth of sculpture, painting, architecture, literature, ceremony and ritual, dance and drama, and music and song. Much of this has been produced in very different times, using very different materials and techniques from those common today. It has also been produced in relative isolation. Today Buddhist culture has been exposed to global culture, meeting influences from many different places and times. It is especially encountering a mass culture that is backed by an almost irresistible commercial force. It is no longer possible to reproduce unselfconsciously the forms of the past and yet it is not at all clear in what direction to look for a Buddhist cultural renewal.

Nonetheless, that quest for new and relevant cultural expressions of the Dharma is of foremost importance if Buddhism is to have a major impact on the world. The Dharma life is not a matter of will and intellect alone. Emotion and, above all, imagination are to be engaged if one is successfully to move forward on the Path. Culture speaks the language of the heart and of the imagination, and, if it expresses Buddhist values, influences the whole of society and enables individuals to practise the Dharma far more effectively.

The development of a contemporary Buddhist cultural expression involves the following considerations:
- Recognising the Dharmic significance of art and culture: Dharmic development naturally expresses itself in a deepening aesthetic sensibility;
- Accepting the potential of artistic creation as a means of Dharma practice, insofar as it reflects the exploration of deeper aspects of experience and leads to self-transcendence;

- Acknowledging the value of ancient Buddhist art and culture, as a source of inspiration, not merely of imitation;
- Appreciating the best of non-Buddhist culture: Great art expresses human values that transcend their context and touch those depths from which the Dharma comes. There are outstanding expressions of human aesthetic sensibility in many other religions, as well as in non-religious art. These can be valued as art, independent of their doctrinal or liturgical associations, and thereby as material for a Buddhist cultural renewal;
- Expressing the rich variety of human experience by embracing the best and most positive aspects of local culture and tradition, so long as it is compatible with the Dharma.

If these principles are applied in depth we can look to the emergence of new Buddhist cultures all over the world, and a strong Buddhist influence on the wider culture. This development will make it possible for more and more people to engage deeply with the Dharma and to live happy and meaningful lives.

V
Going for Refuge to the Sangha

The Sangha *as a refuge* cannot be identified with any human institution or any particular school or tradition. The Sangha Refuge is a basis for complete confidence because it consists of all those men and women down the ages who have gained transcendental insight. Only they can be fully trusted as infallible sources of guidance and example, by virtue of their having seen the way things truly are. When we say, 'To the Sangha for Refuge I Go', it is the Sangha of those who have attained Stream Entry or beyond, the members of the Arya or Bodhisattva Sangha, to which we are committing ourselves. In going for Refuge to the Bodhisattva or Arya Sangha, we are:

- Drawing on the guidance and example of its members;
- Deriving confidence that the Dharma is a true Path to Liberation because there are people who have trodden the Path and realised its goal;
- Gaining inspiration to create the kind of ideal and harmonious society the Sangha represents – a pattern for all human collective life.

All Buddhists today would probably share this understanding of the Sangha Jewel, at least theoretically. However, in some areas of the Buddhist world, the Sangha has come to be identified almost exclusively with the monastic Sangha, whether or not that is explicitly stated. Of course, renunciation is a very important aspect of the Dharma life and those who have gone forth from home into homelessness have opportunities for practising the Dharma that householders will often not have. It should also be stressed that there are many excellent monks and nuns who practise the Dharma wholeheartedly and do their best to spread it vigorously.

Nonetheless, an over-valuation of monasticism often distorts the Buddhist community to the detriment of all. Monks – and, much less commonly, nuns – may then be given honour and economic support regardless of their true worth as spiritual practitioners. So long as they wear the robe and do not too obviously breach the Vinaya, they are likely to be treated as teachers and exemplars. Quite a number therefore do little to deserve the respect and dana they receive and do not contribute much to the practice and spread of the Dharma. The effect on lay people can be equally harmful. Quite a number of lay people have learned that their only role in the Dharma is the support of the monastic Sangha. They believe that by giving dana to the monks they will gain merit, which will help them in this life and the next. This relieves them of responsibility for more intensive practice of the Dharma.

This 'merit economy' can then feed the worldly interests of both lay and monastic, trapping them in a superstitious symbiosis that undermines Buddhist practice. Often this system is tied up with outdated economic and social structures and is thus defenceless in the face of urbanisation, industrialisation, and the growing democratic spirit.

While there are many exceptions to this analysis, both among monks and nuns and among lay people, it is quite commonly true. This notion of Sangha is quite unfit for the task that Buddhism now faces.

The most urgent task for the renewal of Buddhism is the renewal of Sangha.

THE SIGNIFICANCE OF SANGHA
The Arya or Bodhisattva Sangha is our Refuge, but we need Sangha in a more immediate sense. It is very difficult indeed to practise as Buddhists without a social context that is geared to the Dharma. **We need companions on the Path who can encourage and support us at every stage.**

Practising the Dharma is not at all easy, especially because it goes against conventional norms: most people consider that the important issues of life are simply survival, reproduction, and worldly success and they do not hold strongly any ethical or spiritual values – whatever ceremonies they may undertake or offerings they may give. There is seldom much sympathy, outside societies that preserve traditional Buddhist culture, for those who want to live a Dharma life. If we are to make genuine progress on the Path, we need to be in deep connection with those who see things in the same way that we do and who will therefore understand and assist our efforts.

Not only does Sangha give us moral support, it is itself one of the chief arenas for our practice. The purpose of Dharma practice is going beyond our narrow self-attachment, which, according to the Buddha, is the source of all our suffering. We transcend self-attachment by cultivating the selfless emotions of *maitrī* and compassion, not merely in the meditation hall but in our daily lives. The Sangha, in the form of our own immediate circle of Dharma companions, offers us the best opportunity to learn to live and work closely with others in deep and loving harmony. It does so through example and guidance, and through all the practices of Sangha –

notably of confession, which enables us to face up to and overcome our own unskilful actions. Sangha members can mutually reflect each other so that all may discover how to practise the Dharma more deeply. Such an active Dharmic culture within the Sangha ensures that teachings and practices remain truly effective and do not become mere formalities.

Furthermore, a successful Sangha is an example to all of what the whole of society could be. This is very urgently needed in a consumerist world in which there is an increasing erosion of collective life lived on the basis of genuine values. People need to see actual examples of friendship and harmony in a context of high ideals and ethical living, so that they too can have the courage to lead better lives. Not only is a Sangha an example, from it comes guidance and teaching for those who themselves want to lead a Dharma life.

It should also be said that **if a Sangha is a genuine Sangha it will be a source of delight and happiness to all who participate in it.** This is the kind of Sangha the world needs today.

SPIRITUAL FRIENDSHIP

Sangha is a general principle that is put into effect especially through particular relationships between Sangha members. Traditionally the Sangha relationship that has most often been stressed is that between teacher and disciple. Although the relationship with a teacher is a very important one and many examples can be found of its great effectiveness, there is frequently a strong emphasis on its formal aspects, involving little meaningful human contact. It can also be abused, too often being based upon power, rather than on *maitrī*, which from the social point of view is the essence of the Dharma.

What needs to be stressed in a renewal of Buddhism is *kalyāna mitratā*, 'lovely friendship' or 'friendship in the beautiful', which

signifies friendship in the Dharma: whether between more experienced and less so or between those of more or less equal experience. Teacher and pupil should be friends – the Dharma can only truly be taught and practised in this context.

Friendship is a rich and highly desirable human experience that is made all the more precious by being practised in the context of the Dharma. It has a number of components: shared values and ideals, deep sympathy and liking, mutual knowledge and understanding, cooperation and helping one another, and faithfulness. The quality that makes it possible is communication – which is more than the mere exchange of information: it is a mutual awareness and responsiveness, which can take one very far indeed beyond self-attachment. **Indeed communication and friendship are among the most powerful Dharma methods we have – as well as being among the most important and delightful fruits of Dharma practice.**

The experience of friendship and the development of communication are the basis for Sangha. Although organisation is vitally important for the spreading of the Dharma, organisation is secondary to friendship and Sangha. **Organisations will only be Dharmically effective if they are formed out of Sangha.** The very active work that is needed to make the Dharma much more widely known in the modern world needs to be done on the basis of Sangha in a spirit of friendship.

SPIRITUAL COMMITMENT NOT LIFESTYLE IS THE TEST OF SANGHA

Throughout the Buddhist world, the principal distinction within the community is between monastics and householders. But this is not really the most important issue. **The key question is the degree to which an individual Goes for Refuge to the Three Jewels** – to what extent they are genuinely committed to the Buddhist Path. We have already seen that going for Refuge to the Buddha, Dharma, and Sangha is the central and definitive act of the Buddhist life. What makes you a Buddhist is that you actively practise the Dharma in harmony with others as disciples of the Buddha. A Buddhist is one who effectually treads the Path and is thereby making progress towards Buddhahood. This can be done whether or not one is wearing a robe, as is evidenced by the many lay disciples in the Buddha's own time who achieved transcendental attainment. Indeed, many who wear a robe make no effective effort on the Path at all – and many progress spiritually who have never worn a robe.

The Arya or Bodhisattva Sangha apart, the Sangha that is most significant consists of all those who are putting their going for Refuge to the Three Jewels into effect, regardless of whether they are monastic or lay. A sincerely committed monk has far more in common with a sincerely committed laywoman than he does with his monastic brothers who are merely wearing the robe for the sake of the security and status it confers. A renewed Sangha needs to come together on the basis of commitment, not lifestyle.

SANGHA UNITED ON THE BASIS OF COMMITMENT

Commitment is the fundamental criterion for entry into the Sangha, not any other consideration, such as lifestyle, gender, nationality, education, race, or social class or caste. In the first place, this means that there can be no hierarchical distinction between monastics and lay people. **All are equal members of a single Sangha, so long as they are genuinely and effectively committed to the Three Jewels**, in the sense of systematically applying themselves to the practice of the Dharma. 'Sangha' does not merely mean the monastic Sangha – most commonly the Bhikshu Sangha, thereby excluding the nuns – but the community of all those who go for Refuge to the Buddha, Dharma, and Sangha to an effective degree.

This is especially significant as regards the place of women in the Sangha. The traditional Buddhist world generally assigns a lesser place to women: according to all Vinayas, the most senior nun must defer to the most junior monk. These traditions came from social and economic circumstances very different from our own, in which women are able to play a full and equal part in social, cultural, economic, and political life. A renewed Sangha should accept people simply on the basis of their commitment, not their gender – although there may well be situations where men and women wish to live or practise separately, for obvious practical reasons. No superiority, whether spiritually or organisationally, should attach to anyone simply because they are a man or a woman.

The Sangha transcends the categories of the world. Relationships within the Sangha are based on people's commitment, their moral and spiritual worth, not the accidents of nationality, race, or economic class. **The ideal Sangha is one that crosses as many boundaries as possible, so that the status accorded by birth is broken down.** For a modern Sangha, one of the most powerful practices is bringing people together from many different backgrounds, especially internationally, and practising the Dharma together simply as individuals who go for Refuge to the Three Jewels.

SUTRA-STYLE MONASTICISM

While a renewed Sangha would not accord special status to anyone simply on the basis of their lifestyle, nonetheless **renunciation is to be highly valued and supported**: that is, the renunciative lifestyle is to be valued in itself, although the individuals who profess it can only be valued according to their own moral and spiritual worth, not the way of life they profess. Renunciation is essential to the Dharma life: in order to make progress on the Path, one renounces the world as much as possible, with all its enticements to attachment. It is very valuable indeed that some people choose to live without so many of the things that bind most of us into Samsara.

However, monasticism in the Buddhist world is in urgent need of renewal, dominated as it can be by formalism, compromise with authority, and concern with property and even wealth – and at times by outright hypocrisy. Because the following of sets of Vinaya rules, established in quite different historical circumstances, has become the key definer of monasticism, its underlying meaning and purpose is frequently lost. Becoming a monk or nun in reality means renouncing family and possessions so that one can go for Refuge wholeheartedly and with as little distraction as possible. We need a new style of Buddhist monasticism, based not on Vinaya rules, though drawing on their spirit, but on the principles of the Buddha's own way of life, in accordance with modern circumstances.

We need what could be called **'sutra-style' monasticism** – inspired by the way of life of the Buddha's companions as depicted in the early discourses. It is best to be cautious about legislating as to how 'sutra-style' monks and nuns should behave, because circumstances vary so much – and because legislation always offers the opportunity for keeping the letter while breaking the spirit, as is often the case with the following of the Vinaya rules. We can however discern five principles at work in the life of a successful renunciant in this sense:

- **Chastity**: *brahmacharya* is the defining feature of monasticism, but it means more than mere abstention from sexual activity. It refers to a highly positive state of freedom from craving. Those leading a monastic life should not merely be chaste, but should be happily so. Too many monks and nuns either hypocritically compromise their

vows in various ways or else are unhappily chaste, with all the psychological and behavioural consequences that repression can bring;
- **Fewness of possessions**: the 'sutra-style' monk or nun limits what they own to what they immediately and genuinely need for their physical survival and the carrying out of their work for the Dharma;
- **Simplicity of lifestyle**: this is especially important and especially difficult in the complex and busy modern environment. It essentially means eliminating from one's life whatever is unnecessary to Dharma practice, so that one is not wasting one's time on the mere business of accumulation and safeguarding of possessions or in activities that are distractions. Simplicity of lifestyle does not mean deprivation or degradation: a simple life should be healthy and full of uncomplicated, dignified, and inexpensive beauty – an 'elegant simplicity'. It could also be said that this principle, combined with the others, is 'environmentally friendly', for the sutra-style monastic has left the consumerist system that is the primary cause of our current environmental crisis;
- **Careerlessness**: One takes up the monastic life so that one may devote all one's time and energy to the Dharma. One may, of course, need to take paid employment to earn enough to live on, but one's work is not an alternative focus for one's energies or a means of furthering worldly ambition. For those engaged in Buddhist activities, there is a special danger: they should take care not to make a career out of monastic life, channelling ambition into ecclesiastical advancement and power;
- **Community living**: The monk or nun has renounced marriage and family but still needs friendship, emotional warmth, and intimacy. Such social support and engagement will come from those who share the same way of life, living together in residential spiritual

communities. Without this kind of community, it is very difficult to maintain a celibate life and one risks either abandoning it or maintaining it with some degree of emotional and instinctual repression.

Those who take the vow of *brahmacharya* do so in the context of the precepts that all Buddhists should try to follow. They take the vow as a special and more intense practice of the third precept of refraining from sexual misconduct that is common to all. It is important that this is born in mind. Every genuine Buddhist is practising ethics, including in the area of sexual conduct. Indeed, **every Buddhist also needs to live as much as they can by the other principles outlined above: fewness of possessions, simplicity of lifestyle, careerlessness, and, if not community living, then active participation in a Sangha in a context of deep friendship.**

CREATING AN ALTERNATIVE WAY OF LIFE

The changed cultural, social, and economic circumstances of the modern world demand that Buddhists today develop new institutions for living the Dharma life. This is especially important because it is now clear that the way of life in rich countries – a way of life to which people in emerging economies understandably aspire and are rapidly gaining access – is the major driver of our environmental problems and of much geo-political tension. Modern economies depend upon increasing consumer demand to drive economic growth – and that growth requires the use of more energy and resources, which in turn leads to more climate-changing carbon use and more tension-building competition for scarce commodities. It seems that our present way of life is simply not tenable indefinitely. **Buddhists can demonstrate a genuinely alternative way of life that lives lightly on the planet and**

that is more truly satisfying than the deliberately stimulated discontent that is the fundamental basis of our present system.

Despite much in the world today that is problematic for the leading of the Dharma life, it also has advantages that can be exploited in the creation of new Buddhist institutions. The greater flexibility and freedom to be found in many societies today offers new opportunities. Traditionally, Buddhists have only had two options: lay life or becoming a monk or nun. Now, for many people, there is a wider range of possibilities.

It is important that those who are able to lead a monastic life in an authentic way are encouraged and assisted to do so. Nonetheless, there are some, perhaps many, who would like to dedicate themselves to a full time Dharma life, but who cannot observe *brahmacharya* without undue strain or the hypocrisy so common in present monastic Sanghas. For most in that position today, there is no option but to marry, because of prevailing conventions in their societies, yet marriage in such circumstances usually restricts Dharma practice, to a greater or lesser extent. However it is now possible in some areas of the world to live a **'semi-renunciant' lifestyle**, applying the five principles mentioned above much more fully than can be done in a family, yet not as fully as a monk or nun. Whether this is feasible or not depends on prevailing social conventions and economic conditions, but in many countries today it is possible, for instance, to live a community life, without being celibate. It is certainly possible for Buddhists to work together. And a new kind of social life can be created, in which even families work very differently from the current norms. These are new opportunities that Buddhists today are exploring.

It is especially important now to find **alternative living situations**, because of the decay of the traditional family in many cultures and the growth of increasingly isolated family units, which have less and less connection with their neighbours. This 'nuclear family' set-up is often unhealthy for all concerned. Urban life for many all over the world is now often lonely and socially fragmented. These conditions are especially unsuitable for those trying to lead a Dharma life, who need the warmth, support, encouragement, and stimulation of fellow Dharma-practitioners and opportunities for developing deep spiritual friendship. A renewed Buddhism can explore different ways for people to live together: for instance, as already mentioned, semi-monastic residential communities for those who are unmarried but do not wish to take up the practice of *brahmacharya* – whether they might do so at some later stage or not. For obvious reasons, these often work best if they are for men and women separately. There is also the possibility of residential communities for those with families – although, for practical reasons, these are usually more difficult to establish.

One of the most important areas that a modern Buddhism needs to address is **economic life**. Most people spend a large proportion of their lives in paid employment, often in unpleasant, boring, or stressful activity. Furthermore, their work often has no connection with their Dharma life and may even compromise their ethical principles. New business institutions need to be formed that enable committed Buddhists to transform their working lives into spiritual practice. There are a number of principles to be taken into account in establishing such businesses:

- **Right Livelihood:** Whatever activity is undertaken should not breach the ethical precepts and principles laid down by the Buddha in the Noble Eightfold Path;
- **Dana:** The work done should make a genuine contribution to the world, whether by fulfilling some basic need, helping to relieve

suffering, or making a financial surplus that can be used to spread the Dharma;
- **Creativity:** As far as possible the work should be fulfilling for those who engage in it, both for the dana end that it serves and for its own sake;
- **Community:** All working for the enterprise should collectively constitute a Sangha at work, everyone sharing a common spiritual perspective and practice;
- **Spiritual practice:** There should be an effort to transform the work itself into a means of practising the Dharma, promoting mindfulness, emotional positivity, inspiration, and insight into the nature of things, as well as a sense of self-transcending service.

Every Buddhist should aim to fulfil as many of these principles as possible in their own working lives.

A renewed Buddhism needs to offer **an alternative cultural and social life**. The books we read, the films we watch, and the music we listen to all have an effect on our attitudes and understanding. Culture shapes consciousness very powerfully. As we have seen, culture can be a medium for Dharma practice, and at the least can greatly support it. Modern civilisation makes entertainment and distraction available with astonishing ease at a very low cost to a very large proportion of the population. Even very poor people have relatively easy access to multi-channel television and the latest popular songs. Most of what is on offer is of no great cultural worth and indeed often communicates the shallowest of consumerism and the most worldly of values.

Within most countries, more worthwhile culture is available for those that seek it, but a new Buddhism needs to make it easily accessible and to relate it to Dharma life. This should be one of the functions of Dharma centres; the primary purpose of such centres is teaching and practising Buddhism, but they need also to serve a social and cultural function. Those trying to follow the Path need opportunities for gathering with those who share their commitment. And they need opportunities for cultural experience other than the mere entertainment or distraction that fills so much of the media. These Dharma centres should offer access to films, plays, poetry, music, and visual art that communicate the Dharma's truths, albeit not in the formal terms of Buddhism. They should help to educate the aesthetic sensibility of their members, so that they are better able to appreciate artistic experiences of a kind that reveals more of the real nature of things.

One of the most challenging cultural issues facing Buddhists today is the power of modern technology and its influence on human experience. The technology we use has a strong effect on consciousness in various ways, and this needs to be confronted and explored. Modern Buddhism needs to offer guidance on **how to live with technology**, taking advantage of its benefits and avoiding its malign effects. At the same time, a renewed Buddhism needs to use the modern media to get its message across. There is no inherent reason why film, television, radio, and the internet cannot communicate the Dharma. Indeed, the way new communication technology has developed generally makes it easier and cheaper to use. **Buddhists can have a very wide effect if they capture as much space as they can in the new media with items that are well presented, engaging, and genuinely inspiring.**

A renewed Buddhism needs to confront the modern world as it is, with intelligence and resourcefulness. This involves using opportunities that arise in contemporary circumstances to develop a complete way of life based on the Dharma that is a genuine alternative to consumer society. That way of life requires the support of a range of

institutions such as communities, Right Livelihood businesses, and Dharma centres that together constitute a kind of new or model society, in the midst of the wider society – the **nucleus of a new society** worldwide. This has three functions:
- Providing resources for those already committed to the Dharma to make further progress on the path;
- Creating bases for spreading the Dharma much more widely throughout the world;
- Demonstrating alternatives to consumer society that can model what the whole world could become.

In the world today these Buddhist societies within the wider society could be seen as replicating the function performed by monasteries in many traditional Buddhist cultures. They would provide rallying points and points of departure: oases where all may find refreshment and bases from which the entire desert may be made to bloom.

TRANSFORMING THE WORLD

The ultimate aspiration of the Sangha is to turn society everywhere into a new society: to transform the whole world into the land of the Dharma – into a 'Pure Land'. Impossibly distant, even Quixotic, as that goal may be, Buddhists should never rest until it is achieved – traditionally it is said that many have devoted themselves to this task even lifetime after lifetime and there is no reason why Buddhists today should not have that same perspective. In more immediate and practical terms, this means that, once the environments have been established that support the lives and Dharma practice of the committed core, every effort will be given to transforming the surrounding society. This requires us to address very directly the situation all around, actively seeking to change it for the better on the basis of the Dharma.

The first duty in this respect is to make the Dharma available in as clear and accessible a form as possible as widely as possible. We need especially to be appealing to all those who feel some urge for a more meaningful life. Many, many people feel deep disquiet because they lack answers to fundamental questions about life. Many are no longer convinced by the solutions offered by the religions they have grown up with. Many are disillusioned by lives lived merely to meet the expectations of convention. However they lack guidance and encouragement to give their lives to something more fulfilling. The Dharma can feed their hunger and the Sangha can support them in their struggles for a better life. We need to be actively reaching out to as many such people as possible.

If a large number of people do lead a Dharma life in this way to any extent this will have a very big effect on society as a whole. However it is not enough to await that day. **Many everywhere at this moment suffer terribly, through injustice, violence, poverty, exclusion, and prejudice. It is our compassionate duty to help them escape their suffering now.** This can be done in two ways: by giving them the direct material aid they need to meet their difficulties and by helping them to help themselves in the future. Buddhists can do both.

We have before us an important example of the power of the Dharma to transform the lives of the severely disadvantaged. In 1956, millions of Indian 'Dalits' – oppressed people from the lowest castes – converted to Buddhism, under the leadership of Dr B. R. Ambedkar, to escape the stigma of 'Untouchability', to which they had been condemned under the Hindu caste system. In the succeeding fifty years, they have very substantially changed their status because of the courage and confidence that the Dharma has given them.

Poverty and oppression leave people feeling passive and fatalistic, very often, especially when they are taught that acceptance is their religious duty, as for instance those at the bottom of the caste hierarchy are told in India. The most basic message of the Dharma is that we are each responsible for our own future. Of course we cannot be held accountable for being born into poverty or being the butt of others' prejudice but we can determine how we respond to our situation and how we escape our disadvantages. The Dharma directly denies doctrines of natural inequality. One human being is not better than another simply because he or she is born into a wealthier or more powerful class, caste, or race. What makes one human being better than another is their moral worth, not their birth.

The message of the Dharma gives an immediate sense of confidence and of moral self-reliance, without preaching violence or disharmony. This has a very great impact. It gives people the courage to lift themselves out of deprivation and oppression through their own efforts, just as Dr Ambedkar's followers have done since their conversion – which is much more effective in the long term than being helped out by others. This message needs to be heard far more widely by those many people all over the world who are excluded from the benefits of the societies they live in.

The Dharma can help those who are downtrodden to lift themselves up, but Buddhists also need to address the system in which some are forced to suffer at the hands of others. **A renewed Buddhism needs to recognise the nature of society and its own role within it.** Society is sustained not so much by the system by which it is governed or the framework of law by which order is kept – although these have a very significant effect. Even a good constitution and good laws can be corrupted by a bad society. It is the values shared by the majority of citizens, and especially the most influential ones, that are the real determiners of the worth of a society. A just and free society arises because citizens generally value justice and freedom and will themselves act on that basis without the coercion of the law.

Values such as freedom and justice are themselves underlain by more fundamental views about the nature and meaning of human life and of our relationship to one another. The way we understand life determines our values and that guides our behaviour. The view of the greatest number will determine the values that generally prevail and the social relations that will result. **The task of Buddhists is to promote the Dharmic view of life and the values that flow from it.** We can try to inject into the public discussion the Dharmic understanding of the way life really is. We can communicate as widely as possible that actions have consequences in accordance with their skilful or unskilful nature. The law of karma simply describes what happens: it is the moral law that describes how our own actions affect us in the future, just as the law of gravity describes what happens to a stone when it is dropped. For Buddhists, morality is part of the way things are. We need to communicate that perspective as widely as possible.

We also need to communicate that human beings are capable of spiritual growth and that that growth consists essentially in self-transcendence. Such growth for a human being is as essential as it is for a plant – by which it follows that lack of growth is unnatural and will have malign consequences. We grow in accordance with certain laws implicit in the way things are. Our human growth obeys the principle of conditionality: the Path itself is governed by laws. We need simply to apply the laws of growth to our own lives. We will then find ourselves experiencing greater and greater happiness and fulfilment.

The ultimate meaning and purpose of human society is the growth of the individuals within it – growth in creativity, love, compassion, and wisdom. If that growth is taking place among large numbers of people, society will be stable because basic human values will be widely shared, moderating competing interests.

If Buddhism is renewed, it can more easily make its influence strongly felt within societies all over the world, asserting values that promote the well-being of all. This requires that Buddhists have a voice within politics, the media, and the arts. Buddhism could promote values of tolerance and equality, ensuring that no one suffers unnecessarily for the accidents of their birth: race, colour, class, gender, sexual orientation, physical disability. It could promote peace and harmony and a spirit of friendliness and cooperation throughout society. And it could promote culture, learning, and the arts as means to a higher human life.

Buddhism has traditionally worked within whatever political and social system it has found itself, having started in the growing monarchies of the Ganges plain. But it can embrace modern democracy wholeheartedly, because democracy at its best is founded upon values that Buddhism wholeheartedly upholds: respect for every individual regardless of birth, moral freedom and responsibility, social harmony. What is more, democracy needs the Dharma very urgently. If democracy is to be something more than merely an arena of competing self-interest, it needs a shared set of ideals.

The world is increasingly pluralistic and it is less and less possible to found nations on racial or historical-cultural values. There needs to be a larger vision of human existence that animates the democratic process: a vision of the common good in terms that are more than merely material. This the Dharma offers supremely, and it does it basing itself not on belief in revelation or authority, but on an analysis of the nature of life that is accessible to reason and that can be confirmed in experience.

The Dharma breathes the spirit of the age and gives it its best expression. It is our duty to make the Dharma heard.

VI
The principles of a Buddhist renewal

The principles outlined in this manifesto are those upon which the Triratna Buddhist Community is founded and they are the basis upon which we try to work together. Since the foundation of our community, we have had some success in creating the kind of Buddhist movement these principles point to – although there is so much that does not live up to these ideals and so much more to be done.

Even though, inevitably in this short booklet, these principles are set out in brief and without full explanation or argument, we believe that they apply to Buddhism as a whole. We therefore invite dialogue with all Buddhists who share with us the desire to make the medicine of the Dharma as widely available as possible in the modern world and who want to renew the Buddhist tradition so that it can make a substantial difference today. If enough of us are engaged together in this renewal we may be able to make a major contribution to the future of humanity in these critical times.

Print copies of this book are available at:
http://tinyurl.com/buddhistmanifesto
And as a pdf:
http://tinyurl.com/buddhistmanifesto2

For further information please visit:

THEBUDDHISTCENTRE.COM
information and news about the Triratna Buddhist Community

SANGHARAKSHITA.ORG
articles, information, and news about Urgyen Sangharakshita

SUBHUTI.INFO
articles, video, information, and news about Dharmachari Subhuti

WINDHORSEPUBLICATIONS.COM
books by Sangharakshita, Subhuti, and other members of the Triratna Buddhist Order

FREEBUDDHISTAUDIO.COM
talks by Sangharakshita, Subhuti, and other members of the Triratna Buddhist Order

VIDEOSANGHA.NET
videos of talks by Sangharakshita, Subhuti, and other members of the Triratna Buddhist Order.